COLLINS GEM
NTIQUE
MARKS

a mine of information

C000144830

COLLINS GEM
CRICKET

a mine of information

EAT

COLLINS GEM
DOGS

a mine of information

a mine of information

COLLINS GEM
NTERNET

a mine of information

COLLINS GEM
PREDICTING

a mine of information

COLLINS GEM
Ready
REFERENCE

a mine of information

COLLINS GEM
SHARKS

a mine of information

COLLINS GEM
WHALES
& DOLPHINS

a mine of information

COLLINS GEM
WHISKY

a mine of information

COLLINS GEM
WORD
PROCESSING

a mine of information

COLLINS GEM
Your PC

a mine of information

CALLIGRAPHY

The Diagram Group

HarperCollins*Publishers*

HarperCollins*Publishers*
Westerhill Road, Bishopbriggs, Glasgow G64 2QT

A Diagram book first created by Diagram Visual Information
Limited of 195 Kentish Town Road, London NW5 2JU

First published 2001

Reprint 10 9 8 7 6 5 4 3 2 1 0

© Diagram Visual Information Limited 2001

ISBN 0 00 710141-4

Printed in Italy by Amadeus S.p.A.

Introduction

Calligraphy is the craft of writing beautifully. It will take time and patience before you acquire the range of skills which are the hallmark of a good calligrapher.

If you are a beginner, *Collins Gem Calligraphy* gives you all the information you need to get started. It describes basic tools and materials – pens, nibs, inks, paints and types of paper – and it illustrates the skills and strokes needed in three simple writing styles. Confidence, which comes from practice, and understanding the basic structure of the letters gives calligraphy a rhythm and a sense of freedom.

Techniques are shown for displaying work on the page and for duplicating it. Once you have mastered a letterform you can put your skill to use in projects such as labelling, and creating greetings cards and posters. Some more difficult letterforms are illustrated at the end of the book.

4

Contents

1. Basic Materials

In this chapter you will be introduced to various tools and writing instruments which, as a beginner, you are recommended to use. It is important to familiarise yourself with the pens and drawing instruments. This process involves playing with them. Just as children learn naturally through play, so will you! Mastering your tools will give you a basic confidence which will gradually develop as your skills improve.

PREPARING A DRAWING BOARD

If you do not have a drawing board, you can make one.

1 Find a strong, flat board with straight edges. Prop it up at an angle of 45° using bricks or books. Make sure it is firm.

2 Tape three sheets of good thick paper securely to the board to create a firm but 'sympathetic' writing surface.

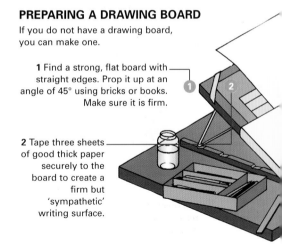

3 Use a sheet of ruled lines as a guide underneath the sheet of paper you are writing on. *(See page 24 for more on ruling.)*

4 Write onto a sheet of layout paper which is not taped down. This paper needs to be free to move upwards as you write down the page, so that your hand stays at the same level on the board at all times.

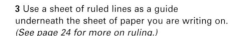

5 Use a sheet of layout paper to protect your work from grease and splatters, etc.

PENS AND NIBS

The next six pages illustrate the variety of writing implements available. They include felt-tip pens, pencils, broad-nibbed pens and fountain pens. The ones marked with an asterisk (*) are the ones you need to start with.

Preparing nibs

New nibs need to be cleaned before use, otherwise the ink will not flow freely. Remove the manufacturer's lacquer from both nibs and reservoirs, either by boiling them in water or by putting them into the flame of a lighted match and then wiping clean.

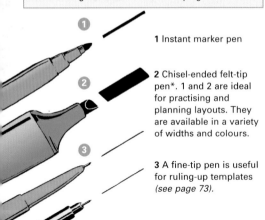

1 Instant marker pen

2 Chisel-ended felt-tip pen*. 1 and 2 are ideal for practising and planning layouts. They are available in a variety of widths and colours.

3 A fine-tip pen is useful for ruling-up templates (see page 73).

4 A carpenter's pencil for practice and experimenting with different layouts.

5 The double pencil* is the most useful dry pen of all. Simply bind two pencils together at the top and bottom with tape or rubber bands to produce an outline pen which shows clearly the letter construction.

To make a broader pen, place an eraser between the two pencils and then bind them together. If you want a narrower pen, shave off some of the wood from the pencils along their length before binding.

6 Chisel-ended felt-tip pen which has had small wedges cut out of the tip with a scalpel, producing a decorative mark.

7 Home-made poster pen. Made by covering a piece of balsa wood with felt and gripping them together in a bulldog clip. This produces an inexpensive pen with a broad nib, which is useful for display work, experimenting, or for children to practise with.

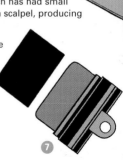

BROAD-NIBBED PENS

8 Reed pen. These can be made from bamboo, honeysuckle or other tubular stems. The reed pen is the original broad-nibbed pen and is ideal for large letters.

9 Synthetic 'reed pen'. Nylon tubing from hardware stores can be made into one. The nib can be cut into to make a pen which produces a double line.

10 A quill. This is made from a cured flight feather of a goose or swan which has been shaped at the end with a sharp knife.

Pens 8, 9 and 10 can be used with added reservoirs *(see page 13)*.

> **Nib widths**
> Nibs are available in an enormous range of widths. The wider the nib, the greater the contrast between the thick and thin strokes produced.

11 The Witch pen has a writing edge which copes very well with textured papers.

12 Boxall Automatic pen. This range includes a variety of nib widths.

13 Boxall Automatic pen with a decorative nib.

14 Scroll nibs are available in sets consisting of a variety of widths, all giving a double line.

15 The Deco Script pen is useful for practising skeleton letters in various sizes.

PENS WITH RESERVOIRS

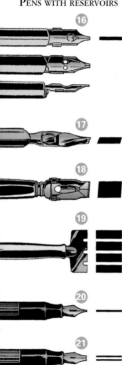

16 William Mitchell Roundhand nib with a slip-on reservoir (top, bottom and side views).

17 Brause nib with reservoir on top of the nib.
You will need either a nib type 16 or 17.

18 Poster pens also have their reservoirs on top of the nib and a right oblique writing edge. This pen is ideal for decorated letters and display work.

19 Coit pens are expensive but have a variety of writing edges producing decorative marks, ideal for display work.

20 Fountain pen*. Using a fountain pen with an Italic nib for your everyday writing will improve it.

21 A shadow fountain pen nib gives two lines. This is ideal for analysing your strokes as well as being decorative.

RESERVOIRS

Reservoirs hold ink on the nib and help to control the ink flow. There are five basic types:

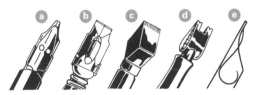

a This reservoir slips underneath the nib and forms a shallow cup shape which just touches the slit. It should not force the slit open. This type is easily removed for cleaning.

b Similar to (**a**) but sits on top of the nib and can also be removed for cleaning.

c The shape of this nib creates its own reservoir. Work with the hairlines on the writing edge facing upwards, as these help control ink flow. Clean the nib by passing a soft cloth between the two 'blades'.

d Coit pen reservoir. These occasionally need to be taken apart to be cleaned.

e (cross section) This reservoir is made from a piece of aluminum from a soft-drink can. Cut the metal into small strips, bend into an S shape and tuck into the barrel of your reed or nylon pen (such as pens 8 and 9 on page 10).

INK, PAINT AND PAPER

As well as selecting a writing implement, you must also
consider the ink or paint and the type of paper you will
use with your pen. Experiment with different
combinations of ink, paper and writing board angle to find
out what suits you best.

When choosing ink, always make sure it is non-
waterproof. Waterproof inks contain gum which will clog
your pen. It is a good idea to keep pots of ink and paint
labelled so that you know exactly what you have.

Inks

1 Ordinary permanent
black fountain ink is the
best ink to start off with.

2 Black Indian
ink is good for
finished work
as it is dense
and very
black.

3, 4 and **5** There are many
other types of ink on the
market. Experiment with
different colours.

Paint

6 Gouache. A few basic gouache paints (designer colours) will give a new dimension to your work. The following colours would be useful to have: zinc (Chinese) white, cobalt blue, lemon yellow, emerald oxide of chromium (mix in lemon yellow to give it body), spectrum red or vermilion hue.

7 A mixing dish for preparing paint. If you already have watercolours you can use them and add zinc white to give opacity to your letters when it is appropiate.

8 Use old, cheap brushes for mixing paint and for transferring paint from the mixing dish to the nib. If the brushes have long handles, shorten them to prevent accidents.

9 A dropper bottle filled with water is ideal for mixing paint. Always add the water to the paint drop by drop. If you are using paint for a long piece of work, you will need to add drops of water occasionally to compensate for evaporation.

PAPER

You will probably use a great deal of paper so you will need to locate a good art shop or a specialist paper supplier so that you can stock up from time to time. Good paper is worth paying extra for, but only buy small quantities until you find which ones you like. You need to consider three main factors when choosing paper: weight (thickness), surface texture ('tooth') and finish (absorbency).

- When you buy a new paper, write the name and other details in a corner, so that you can easily re-order it if you find you like using it.

- Experiment with different paper, ink and pen combinations. To begin with, buy an A3 layout pad. This is an inexpensive, translucent, lightweight paper which you can use for practice and pasting up. Guidelines placed underneath will show through.

- Some good-quality drawing paper is very useful so try a few different weights, then stock up with ones you like. Parch marque is a substitute for parchment and is ideal for making a finished piece look interesting. Fabriano paper, made from cotton, comes in several weights and is very good to use.

PAPER SIZES

A5

Metric	148 x 210 mm
Imperial	5⁷/₈ x 8¹/₄ in
Nearest US equivalent	5¹/₂ x 8¹/₂ in

A4

Metric	210 x 297 mm
Imperial	8¹/₄ x 11³/₄ in
Nearest US equivalents	8¹/₂ x 11 in; 9 x 12 in

A3

Metric	297 x 420 mm
Imperial	11³/₄ x 16¹/₂ in
Nearest US equivalents	11 x 14 in; 14 x 17 in; 11 x 17 in; 12 x 18 in

A2

Metric	420 x 594 mm
Imperial	16¹/₂ x 23¹/₂ in
Nearest US equivalents	18 x 24 in; 19 x 24 in

GOOD WORK PRACTICE

Caring for your equipment
It is good practice to clean pens and brushes immediately after use. This will help to lengthen their useful life and keep them ready for use. Always keep pencils sharp. Your writing tools should be kept in a safe place where they are unlikely to become damaged. Do not allow others to use them.

Setting up a work station
Consider creating a calligraphy workstation in your home.

You will need:
1 A source of natural light and a desk lamp.

2 Space to keep tools and equipment within easy reach.

3 Space to store work. (You may prefer to keep work in a portfolio or put it under the bed between sheets of card.)

4 A comfortable adjustable chair.

5 A drawing board, preferably adjustable *(see pages 6 and 7)*.

6 A steady, strong, flat table on which to put the drawing board.

7 Jars or cutlery tray to store pens and brushes without damaging them.

POSTURE

Body weight should go through the spine. Legs and both feet should rest squarely on the floor. Avoid weight going forward into the arms.

This position should give you:

- Steady ink flow

- A good view of your work

- A relaxed working posture which will not tire you

LEFT-HANDED CALLIGRAPHERS

Here are some hints for left-handed calligraphers to make lettering easier:

1 Left oblique nibs can be purchased. If required, the angle of the nib can be increased by rubbing with FINE silicon carbide paper.

2 Tilt the paper or steepen the angle of the drawing board to make yourself more comfortable.

3 Keep work to the left-hand side of your board. Turn your head a little to the left and don't write across your body – only as far as your chin. Keep your elbow tucked into your waist.

2. Getting Started

The letterform is the 'hand' or style in which you write the letters of the alphabet. Chapter 3 shows three simple letterforms – Skeleton, Foundational and Italic – but

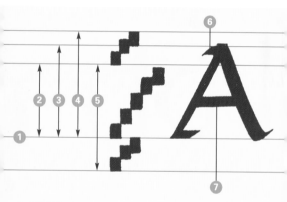

Terms used in Calligraphy	**1** Writing line
Majuscules are upper-case (capital) letters.	**2** x-height (height of minuscules)
	3 Majuscule (capital) height
Minuscules are lower-case (small) letters.	**4** Height of ascenders

before you put pen to paper you will need to familiarise yourself with the terms used in calligraphy.

5	Depth of descenders	11	Counter
6	Serif	12	Foot serif
7	Cross-bar	13	Arch
8	Stem	14	Bowl
9	Ascender	15	Hairline
10	Descender		

PREPARING THE PAPER

LADDERS

The height of each style of letterform is set at a specific number of nib widths, so the size of your lettering is related to the width of the nib you use and the nib itself acts as a measuring unit for the height of the letters. The nib widths are made with a pen angle of 90° and are piled up in a formation known as a ladder.

You must make a new ladder each time you use a different size of nib or change lettering style. In this way, whichever size nib you use, your letters will always be in the correct proportions.

Foundational minuscules (**1**) are 4½ nib widths high and the majuscules 6 nib widths. Italic minuscules (**2**) use 5 nib widths and the Italic majuscules are 7.

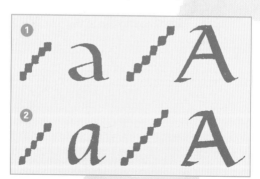

GUIDELINES

Guidelines are lines which act as a guide for the
proportions of the letterforms. These proportions are
found by making a ladder and then ruling pencil lines
from it. They can either be fine pencil lines ruled on the
writing sheet itself or templates placed under the writing
sheet so that the lines show through. It is a good idea to
draw a template to the correct size for each of your nibs.
Templates for some of the letterforms shown in the book
are given on pages 182–85.

PEN PLAY

It is essential to feel at ease when you are learning calligraphy. Get used to the feel of the pen by drawing with it. Here are some patterns based on letterforms.

PEN ANGLES

The pen angle is the angle between the flat edge of the nib and the horizontal writing line. This varies depending on which letterform you are writing.

90° for ladders   30° for Foundation hand   45° for Italic

CORRECTING MISTAKES

Even the best calligraphers make the occasional error!

1 The wrong area can be gently scraped or sliced off with a razor blade and the surface refinished with a burnisher.

2 Artwork for the printer can be tidied up with typing correction fluid or process white paint.

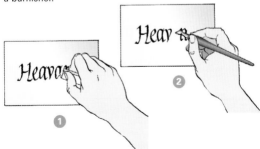

LOOKING AT LETTERS

The Skeleton alphabet is ideal for practising letter shapes and letter spacing, because it is so simple faults are easy to spot. The shapes of letters fit into four groups, each with a similar shape and the same proportions.

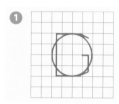

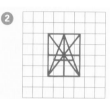

1 C D G O Q are based on a circle. D and G use the edge of the rectangle.

2 A H N T U V X Y Z all fit into a rectangle. Note that the crossbars on A and H are at different heights.

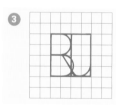

3 B E F J K P R S use half a square. Curves in the lower section need to be a fraction larger to stop letters looking top-heavy.

4 M fits into a square and W (double V, not double U!) is the widest letter. I is the narrowest.

SPACE BETWEEN LETTERS

When spacing letters, you have to take the shape of the
adjoining letters into account. Regular spacing – that is,
leaving the same-size gap between each letter – does not
give the best result. Instead you have to balance the areas,
not the distances, between letters.

Hints for well-balanced lettering

1 Leave a large gap between the two verticals.
2 Put one vertical and one round letter closer
  together.
3 Put two round letters even closer together.

VISUAL SPACING
The counter is the space within the rectangle defined by a letter. Some letters with large counters can be virtually butted up, as their very different shapes make it impossible to confuse them. For instance, an upper-case A and T next to each other look too far apart when their counters are entirely separated (**1**); these letters can be moved very close together without looking strange (**2**).

The larger the letterform the smaller the relative letter spacing can be: the large size of the forms makes them easy to recognise without their own area of white space around them (**3**).

WORD SPACING

When you are writing only a few well-spaced words of showcase lettering, the spacing between the words follows much the same rules as the spacing within words.

If you are doing a long passage of text in a rather smaller size, however, you will not want to fiddle about balancing each and every word with its predecessor. A good general rule is to leave the space of a lower-case n between words in lower case (**4**), and the space of an upper-case O when writing capitals (**5**).

④ *the n quick n brown*
fox n jumps n over
the n lazy n dog

⑤ WEEP THEIR BURDEN
THERE IS ONLY
THE TRAVEL
DENEN ES VON DEN GÖTTERN

3. Simple Letterforms

THE SKELETON LETTERFORM

The Skeleton letterform is the most basic form of letters
and is the first lettering style to learn. The Skeleton letters
can be made with any implement as they do not rely on
the 'thick and thin' effect of a broad-nibbed pen. For this
reason no pen angle or ladder (*see page 24*) is needed. You
can make the letters as large or as small, thick or thin as
you wish. The other two letterforms shown in this chapter,
Foundational and Italic, require a broad-nibbed pen.

To practise drawing the majuscules, divide them into four
groups based on their relative shapes and draw each one
using squared paper (*see page 28*). This way you will learn
how one Skeleton letter differs from the next.

he picol fia, che al meno e

ran testimonio della diuot

nificentia. Alla buona g

ey, and all th

e of Elah, fig

d David ros

e p sempre essere al mod

mia uerso di uostra Ma

ia della qualle humilmete

SKELETON MAJUSCULES

When you practise drawing Skeleton letters, remember
that they are all based on combinations of the straight line

and the circle. Follow the stroke order indicated in the diagrams for a smoother outline.

SKELETON MINUSCULES
The x-height of the minuscules (lower-case letters) should
be half the height of the majuscules (upper-case letters);

the height of the ascenders should equal the height of the majuscules. Numerals are formed slightly higher or lower than the x-height.

THE FOUNDATIONAL HAND

The Foundational hand is the name given by the
calligrapher and typographer Edward Johnston to the
style he developed in the early years of this century. It is
based on his study of the Ramsay Psalter, a 10th-century
Carolingian manuscript in the British Museum. This
minuscule alphabet is used with majuscules based on
the classic Roman capitals. They keep the same
proportions and quality of balance that the original
stonecut letters had.

Ladder and pen angle

The hand has an x-height of 4¹/₂ nib widths (**1**), with an
ascender height of 7 nib widths (**2**), and a capital height
of 6 nib widths (**3**). The basic shape is the round O and
the letters stand vertically without a slope. The hand is
written with the pen at 30° (**4**) to the writing line, except
in the case of some of the capital letters when several
changes in pen angle must be made.

FOUNDATIONAL MAJUSCULES

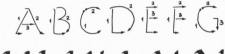

Changing pen angle

The pen angle used is 30° (**1**), but there are a few exceptions to this. The diagonal strokes are steepened to 45° (**2**), and occasionally the pen is flattened to a mere 5° (**3**) in order to maintain a harmonious look.

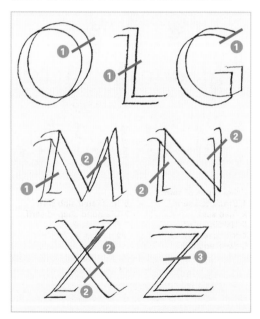

Serifs

Serifs give a finish to a pen stroke. The triangular serif (**a**) is particularly elegant, while the slab serif (**b**) gives added power to a letter and is used on capitals only.

Other types of serif

1 Bracketed serif
2 Slab serif
3 Hairline serif
4 Wedged serif
5 Swelled stroke
6 Bracketed slab serif
7 Diamond-shaped serif
8 Cross-stroke
9 Clubbed serif

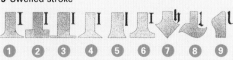

MINUSCULES LETTER GROUPS

Before you start to write out the alphabet, look first at the groups of letters. They are grouped according to their shape and it is easier to stick to one basic shape at a time.

1

Group 1 The O shape
Work around from 11 o'clock to 5 o'clock, first anticlockwise, then clockwise. Follow the stroke order from the alphabet diagrams opposite.

2

Group 2 The arch shape
Note how it relates to the O and is not angular at all.

3

Group 3 The inverted arch, the u shape
I and t both have stable bases to sit on.

4

Group 4 Diagonals
The angle is steepened for these strokes, otherwise they would spread too wide.

5

Group 5 The remaining letters
The shapes of these letters have little in common, but all need individual attention during construction.

FOUNDATIONAL MINUSCULES

abcdefghijk

abcdefghijk

lmnopqrstu

lmnopqrstu

vwxyz gx yy

vwxyz gx yy

1234567890

1234567890

PRACTISING FOUNDATIONAL

The nature of practice is that while it is very necessary, it
can be boring! Here are some ideas for you to work on
and develop while you practise the Foundational hand. Do
not be tempted to rush on and try Italic at this stage.
There are several differences between these two hands that
may confuse you. Before you leave the Foundational hand,
write out a small quotation.

DOODLING

Doodling does not need concentration and can be very
relaxing. Try to keep your pen at the correct angle.

WORDS

Go through the alphabet using a short word for each letter. Continue even if some words look very bad. The aim is to keep writing and fill a sheet or two with words. Repeat the task using names instead of words.

ABLE · BAT · CAT · DOG ·
I suggest experimenting with
EGG · FISH · GET · HIGH ·
capitals, serifs & lower case using
ICE · JOE · KATE · LION ·
different nib sizes, remembering
MAN · NUT · ORBIT ·
that nib widths are the measur-
PIP · QUILL · RAT · STY ·
ing unit for letter height & you
TOP · UNITY · VIEWS ·
aim for roundness and check for
WOW · X-RAY · YOUNG
even spacing by reversing the page
& ZEST · EXERCISES!

Foundational example
A student's early attempts are shown here to demonstrate some of the problems you might be experiencing.

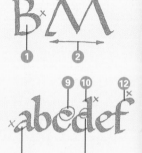

Problems
- With majuscules (capitals), keep the lines straight or circular.
- Don't invent swoops and curves.
- Don't go too low before you arrive at the halfway mark on the letters P R F E K B. Check the proportions by turning the page upside down – constructional mistakes are easily revealed with this simple procedure.
- Try not to be over-critical.

1 Bottom bowl too wide
2 Feet are splayed out too wide so alter angle to 45°; remember the square
3 Side strokes too thick; need to change pen to 45° angle
4 Lost control! 45° angle needed
5 This lacks confidence; a good attempt

6 Too wide; 45° angle needed. Blots and smudges are a beginner's hazard. Stroke 4 pushed up instead of pulled down

7 A weak middle stroke; flatten the pen angle here

8 Wrong proportions

9 Too curved

10 Clumsy serifs

11 Bad join between two strokes

12 Too hooked

13 Control lost

14 Dot too comma-like

15 Hook far too big

16 Leg stroke too long

17 Wobbly arches

18 Too heavy

19 Poor curve

THE ITALIC HAND

The Italic hand was developed in Italy during the Renaissance. There were famous writing masters then as well as many artists and craftsmen, and we still refer to their teaching examples today. There are several different versions of Italic: formal, informal, pointed, cursive and chancery.

Additionally, it can be compressed, extended, flourished and decorated. It is the most flexible of all the calligraphic hands.

All Italic hands share two basic characteristics – the branching arches and the elliptical stress – which make them faster to write than round hand. Don't try to speed up when you write; think instead of the shapes and the rhythm; speed will come later.

Ladder and pen angle

Italic minuscules have a 5 nib width x-height (**1**) with 8 nib widths for the ascenders (**2**) and 8 for the descenders (**3**).The majuscules have a 7 nib width height (**4**). The pen is held at 45° to the writing line and all letters slant to the right no less than 5° from the vertical (**5**).

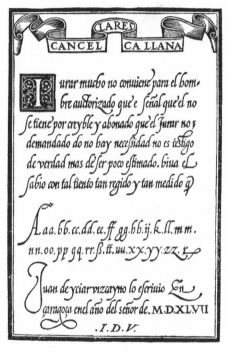

A page from Juan de Yicar's *Arte Subtilissima*, 1550, Saragossa, Spain.

PEN PLAY

The simple pen exercises shown below will give you a 'feel' for the Italic hand.

ITALIC MINUSCULES

Practise the pen play exercises first before working through the minuscule alphabet shown overleaf. Use your double pencil (*see page* 9) the first time and concentrate on the 45° pen angle. Try to maintain it happily throughout an 11 x 14 in (A3) sheet of mark-making exercises.

CHANGING PROPORTIONS

The Italic hand lends itself to decoration. Descenders and
ascenders can be extended and flourished (*see page 56*).
When you are more confident you can try this by changing
the proportions when ruling up and allowing extra space
above and below the x-height.

If you are writing out a poem, or anything with more than
three or four lines, keep your ascenders and descenders
controlled as they can interrupt the flow of the whole
piece if they are too long. On the other hand, elegance and
charm can be added to Italic by increasing ascenders and
descenders. You will soon learn when that would be
appropriate.

ITALIC MINUSCULES

ITALIC MAJUSCULES

FLOURISHING ITALIC

Flourishes are extensions to ascenders, descenders and capital letters, and on the last letter of a line or a word. They are either alive, ribbon-like and effective, or tight, too condensed and distracting, so it is important to experiment and feel confident about making them. Over-ornate flourishes are attention-seeking and fussy, whereas successful ones delight the eye. Start with simple ribbons and aim to use them sparingly. Think of it as flicking a ribbon or cracking a whip, not as an ornate pattern.

Four ways to flourish
1 On an initial letter
2 On the ascenders
3 On the descenders
4 As the finishing stroke
  of a word

Single strokes
Some flourishes can be made in one stroke:
1 A simple ribbon-ink flourish

2 A whipcrack flourish

A part of the word
The flourishes below are from the ends of words and look like natural extensions of the letters. Beware of making flourishes look too 'busy'.

VARIATIONS

These pages show some examples of flourishes on
descenders and ascenders.

1. They should be free-flowing and rhythmic, but also
   depend on where the word appears in your work and
   the emphasis you want to put on it.

2. Over-ornate flourishes can look contrived and do not
   flow freely. They distract from the word and appear
   to seek attention. In these examples the flourishes,
   although ornate, are balanced by the exaggerated
   height of the ascender.

3. Parallel strokes and diagonal stress give emphasis to
   a word.

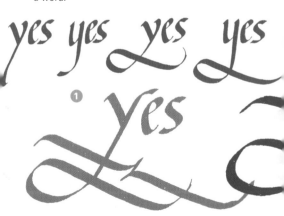

italic

brave

Amen

VARIATIONS OF ITALIC

Italic is a generic term which covers all the variations of the style. The letterforms are formed in just the same way as formal Italic (*see pages 52–55*), but changing the proportions, condensing or opening out the letters, or making them more angular or rounded, creates endless variations on the theme.

Angular Italic

This lower-case Italic has an angular and spiky quality with hairlines on some ascenders and descenders.

Arrighi's Italic

The piece of work opposite is an extract from the work of Ludovico Arrighi, a Venetian scribe, and was published in 1533. Arrighi published several books of writing examples and his copy books using the cursive hand had a great influence on the development of the Italic hand.

Seguita lo essempio delle lre che pono
ligarsi con tutte le sue seguenti, in tal mo-
do cioe

aa ab ac ad ae af ag ah ai ak al am an
ao ap aq ar as at au ax ay az
Il medesmo farai con d i k l m n u.
Le ligature poi de' c f s ſ t sonno
le infra=
scritte

ct, ſa ff ſi fm fn fo fr fu fy,
ſt st

ſſ ſſ ß ſt, ta te' ti tm tn to tq tr tt tu
tx ty
Con le restanti littere De lo Alphabeto, che
sono, b e g h o p q r x y z z
non si deue' ligar mai lra
alcuna seguente

Decorated Italic
This Italic alphabet (*right*) uses elegant, free-flowing
extensions of the letters known as swashes. The capital
can be used to give vitality and charm to a piece of
writing. The light and spacious quality is made by
extending the ascender and the descender height of the
minuscules, and opening out the capitals. The lettering
should stand on its own without unnecessary additional
decoration.

Experiment yourself by taking a few lines of text and write
it out in different variations of Italic, condensing,
extending or adding flourishes or hairlines as you wish.
Compare the same piece written in decorated Italic and in
angular Italic. The overall moods of the two pieces will be
surprisingly different.

abcdefghijk
lmnopqrstuvwx
yzß&&ſt
ABCDEFGH
IJKLMNO
PQRSTU
VWXYZ

ITALIC HANDWRITING

As you begin to develop your calligraphic skills you might like to consider ways of adapting your handwriting. Italic handwriting is a rhythmic and legible way to write beautifully all the time. Use it as often as possible, for writing cheques, notes, lists, memos, etc. The Italic handwriting alphabet is shown on pages 68 and 69. The exercises below are to help you practise the rhythmic movements that are needed for Italic handwriting. With practice, it is possible to write quickly and effectively in Italic in only a few weeks, but concentrate on shape and rhythm before attempting to increase your speed.

Do not confuse Italic handwriting with formal Italic script. If you feel this is beginning to happen, stop practising one and concentrate solely on the other for a while.

Points to remember

- The x-height of the letters is 5 nib widths. The height of the ascenders and descenders is 9 nib widths. The height of the majuscules is 7 nib widths.

- Italic handwriting uses ligatures – strokes which join one letter to another to give a continuous, fluent script. For most of the time, the pen stays in contact with the paper.

- The pen should be held at an angle of 45° to the writing line to maintain the correct distribution of thick and thin lines.

- Try not to press hard with the pen; unnecessary pressure when making upwards strokes can slow you down and cause the ink to splatter.

- If you are left-handed you should use an oblique nib. It helps if you adjust the paper sideways a little and keep your left elbow tucked well in.

ITALIC HANDWRITING MINUSCULES

h i j k l m

h i j k l m

t u v w x y z

t u v w x y z

ITALIC HANDWRITING MAJUSCULES

G H I J K L

G H I J K L

R S T U V

R S T U V

Handwriting exercises

1 45° mountains, with thin upwards and thick downwards strokes.

2 Springing arches in the proportion 2:3.

3 Swinging-up pattern.

4 The pull-down stroke, the arch and the ligature (joining stroke).

5 Letters that can be made in one stroke: o, c and e.

6 Go through the alphabet with m as a middle letter, remembering to keep the 2:3 proportion.

ama ama
bmb bmb
cmc cmc

7 Lift the pen after these letters: b, g, j, p, q, s, x, y. Lift the pen before these letters: a, c, d, g, f, z.

se be pe
je ye

8 Check the pen angle if your letters look wrong: (**a**) too steep, (**b**) too flat, (**c**) correct.

abc abc abc

(a) (b) (c)

4. Templates and Techniques

This chapter is concerned with the various technical skills you will need in order to do the projects in the next chapter. Designing a piece of work, developing the colour scheme, pasting it up and possibly experimenting with changing the weight, style or size of the letters are all familiar tasks to the graphic designer.

TEMPLATES

A template is a design aid. It is a basic pattern which helps you to make accurate repeats of the same shape. Guidelines (*see page 25*) are a form of template. Make several copies by tracing them off or by using a photocopier. Some copiers have an enlarging and reducing facility, which can be used to make copies at a variety of sizes. Templates can save a great deal of time and reduce the risk of inaccuracy.

Plastic templates can help when drawing both regular and free flowing curves. They can be bought from art shops. They are useful, but they may be expensive, so only buy ones you know you will use!

1 Triangles (set squares)
2 French curves
3 A flexicurve – plastic-
   coated wire which will
   bend to any shape
   you wish

4 Ellipses
5 Circles
6 Protractor for angles
   and arcs

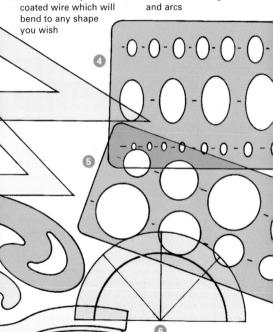

CUTTING A SILHOUETTE

A silhouette template, cut from a piece of card, can be used to great effect. Using a line template along with a shape template can help a great deal when doing 'production-line' projects such as Christmas cards.

Draw a template (**1**) and cut it out (**2**). Create your design using the shape template and a line template (**3**).

WRITING LINES

These can be a very useful guide for letter proportions if you draw them to the correct size for your nibs. They can also be used as a guide for writing in a straight line, to measure space between lines of writing and for making up page layouts.

CENTRING

Centring lines of lettering will immediately make a piece of work look much more professional. The effort you have to make is well worth it. Centring can be used for poems, posters, cards or page layout, as well as for menus.

It is very flexible as it works well with plain letters or with flourishes and illustrations. You should aim for symmetry, both of content and space, so experiment by moving lines closer together or further apart.

Procedure

1 Write out individual lines of writing with some variation in nib size.

2 Cut out the lines just above ascenders and just below descenders. You can cut close to your capitals (**a**).

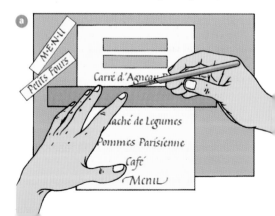

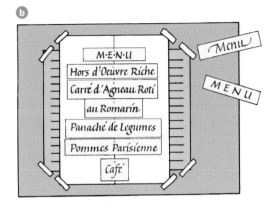

3 Place a line template with a vertical line drawn through the centre under a sheet of layout paper. Tape them at the corners.

4 Measure out each line of letters and mark the half-way point with a dot.

5 Lay the lines of writing out in the correct order with the centre marks over the vertical line on your template (**b**).

6 Begin to experiment with the various options. Move lines closer together and further apart. Imagine that, instead of a series of labels, you are looking at one piece of work. Try to ignore the edges of the labels. Squinting through your eyelashes helps a little! It may be necessary to rewrite some words.

7 When you think it looks balanced, secure each piece of paper with a tiny amount of paper glue (**c**). Place a piece of glass over the whole thing (use some from an old picture frame, if possible). The weight of the glass flattens the paper and makes words read more clearly.

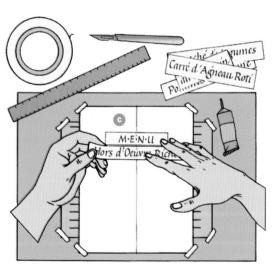

8 Make more adjustments if necessary. Place pieces of card in a neutral colour around the edges to judge the correct amount of space around the words (**d**). Remove the glass and mark the cornerpoints. Do a final paste-up when you are satisfied, sticking the labels firmly to the layout paper. Measure with dividers for accuracy.

9 Place this rough version on top of a piece of good paper and, using a pin, prick through at the ends of each line.

10 Write out carefully, but try not to tense up because it will show in the letters. Relax and enjoy the writing.

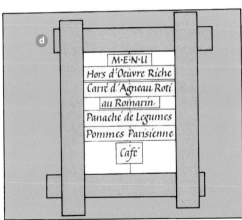

M·E·N·U

Hors d'Oeuvre Riche

Carré d'Agneau Roti
au Romarin

Panaché de Legumes

Pommes Parisienne

Café

LETTER AND WORD SPACING

Letter spacing will depend on what style you are using. In general, allow only enough space for the word to flow, and remember that the space between any two letters should be governed by their shape and not by strict rules of maintaining a set distance between them (*see page 30*).

Between words you need only allow space equivalent to a letter 'n'. Any more, and you may find that, on half closing your eyes, 'rivers' of space (**a**) run down between the words.

the quick brown
fox jumps over
the lazy dog

LETTER FITTING

When a typesetter finds that a line is too long, he can adjust the letter spacing so that the words are more spread out or closer together. Calligraphers use other devices, including changing the letter size, overlapping letters, sharing stems, and placing letters within each other. These are all traditional options which add charm and individuality to a piece of work. Remember to reduce your nib size so that the smaller words have a pleasing proportion and match the rest of the text.

In many ancient manuscripts, small letters are fitted inside or alongside larger ones. Looping letters together was another way of squeezing them into a smaller space.

LINE SPACING

Generally, a distance of twice the x-height (**a**) between the lines of writing will guarantee that ascenders and descenders from one line will not touch the ascenders and descenders of the lines above and below it (**b**). On regularly ruled paper or guidelines this will simply mean using every third line as your writing line, the one above acting as the guideline for the x-heights of the letter.

Increase this standard line spacing when using flourishes, swashes, decorated letters or styles which have elongated ascenders and descenders.

angling is a popular
sport for children

angling is a popular
sport for children

SPACING CAPITALS

Large headings written in capitals can be very effective.
Space between lines of capitals can be reduced. In a short
instruction or message it is the space around the letters
which must be maintained.

1 A clear statement.

2 Shouting at the reader!

3 Wrong, because the
reader 'reads' the space in
the middle.

WE ARE
CLOSED

WE ARE

CLOSED

WE ARE

CLOSED

ALIGNMENT

Alignment refers to whether the left-hand or right-hand edges of your lettering line up – or whether they both do or neither. Text which is aligned on both the right and the left is said to be justified. The alignment can be used sometimes to express formality or informality. For instance, it might be appropriate to do a citation for valour in a block which is justified left and right, and an informal invitation to an open house in a seemingly casual asymmetric alignment.

Types of alignment
The five basic styles of lettering alignment are illustrated here:

1 Justified – both left-hand and right-hand edges line up with each other.
2 Centred – lines are uneven in length, but symmetrical down the centre.
3 Ranged left, ragged right.
4 Ranged right, ragged left.
5 Asymmetric – the lines are not aligned and are freely positioned.

THE VICTORIA & ALBERT MUSEUM

An example of an asymmetric variation.

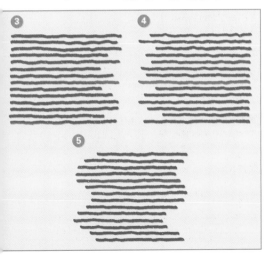

SLANT AND STRESS

Two characteristics that are very important in lettering are slant and stress. Once you have learned to identify the slant and stress of a particular letterform, it will be much easier to imitate it. Both characteristics are constant within a well-designed letterform; for instance, if one upright stroke is perpendicular, so should the others be. If one letter is written with the pen at an angle of 40°, then all the letters in that face should be written with the pen at the same angle.

WORD SLANT

In a consistent letterform, there will be a rhythm within the letters when they are formed into words. All of the main uprights, ascenders, descenders, etc., will be at the same angle. This is one of the features to pay very careful attention to, as consistency in slant is one of the main characteristics of good lettering.

Brighton Brighton

Brighton Brighton

Brighton

STRESS

Stress is the internal angle of the letterform, and refers to the angle at which the tool making the letters is held. Stress is not necessarily related to slant. To discover the different stresses that can occur in letterforms, tie two pencils together and draw a letter U as shown.

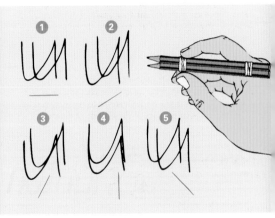

1 Upright or vertical stress made with pencils held horizontally.
2 Pencils angled anticlockwise at 30°.
3 Pencils angled anticlockwise at 60°.
4 Horizontal stress made with pencils held vertically.
5 Pencils angled clockwise at 45°.

INITIAL LETTERS

Initial letters are a dramatic way of livening up a plain piece of lettering, or of providing the opportunity for an extra-fancy piece of penmanship. Very elaborate initial letters should be used sparingly; their best use is as a single decoration at the start of a piece of work. Less elaborate large letters can be used for the beginning of names, or at the start of a new paragraph – or to begin each line if you have a list.

VISUAL SPACING

When the initial letter has straight sides, such as N or H, there is no difficulty over where to start the lines of lettering. However, when there is a large counter, such as with V, R, L or K, the lettering looks better if it is moved in to fill up the counter. This is also true to a lesser extent of B, O, F and similar letters.

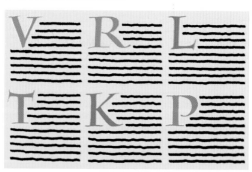

Drop capitals

Drop capitals are outsize capital letters that are 'dropped' into the text below, so that they take up space that would normally be filled with lettering. Simple drop capitals may take up only one extra line; more elaborate forms may eat into many lines, or even a whole page.

Swashes

Swashes can look very effective when used on initial letters for single words, names, etc. Make sure you have enough room to do the swashes unhampered by later lettering.

Pen

Vanya

PAGE LAYOUT

Page layout is an art in itself; the look of the final page can be just as important as the quality of the actual lettering. The aim is to achieve a page that looks well balanced; not too crowded, not with all the elements on one side, and not with too much white space around the work. Use lots of pages in your sketchbook to experiment with different ideas. Be bold and inventive once you have grasped the basic principles of page layout; you might discover some unusual layouts that will look stunning when they are worked up into finished calligraphy.

Traditionally, Bibles and religious texts have been written in columns. This is an ideal way of putting a lot of writing on one page. If you are writing a book consider the effect of both left and right pages together.

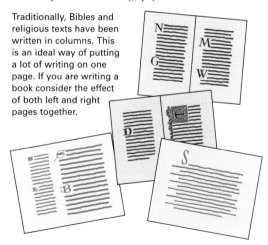

MARGINS

Margins – the spaces left around the edges of the lettering area – are the main elements to consider when you are planning your page layout.

1 The margins are too large; the lettering looks lost in the middle.

2 The margins are too small, the lettering is crowding the page.

3 The margins are just right and balance the lettering area.

ASYMMETRIC LAYOUTS
Many page designs are
slightly – or noticeably –
asymmetric. Rather than
having the lettering
placed in the
mathematical centre,
asymmetric designs are
more pleasing to the eye.
The layouts can be as
restrained or as bold as
you like: experiment with
several different
proportions.

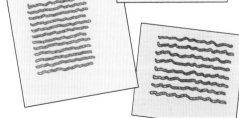

PLEASING PROPORTIONS

Over the years, classic proportions have been worked out for the placing of a regular block of text with margins around it. One set of margin proportions is shown on the right; they are 6 units at the bottom, 3 units at the top, 2 units at one side and 5 units at the other.

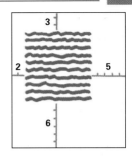

DOUBLE COLUMNS

Sometimes you will want to do two columns of lettering on one page. The columns may be exactly the same size, or one may be smaller or more irregular than the other. These examples show only some of the double-column layouts possible.

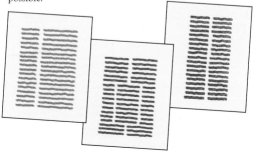

UNUSUAL LAYOUTS

Historical manuscripts and various cultural sources can provide ideas for unusual layouts. Shown below are some of the many possibilities.

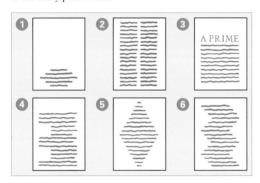

1 Use space to focus attention onto the letters. This device is frequently used in Eastern art.

2 If you have a large text, try splitting it into two columns. Bibles and some secular manuscripts were often done this way.

3 Embellish the opening of your text with large words. This was often done in Bibles and manuscript books.

4 Stagger the work quite freely. This would be appropriate for a humorous quotation or a lyrical rhyme.

5 and **6** Use geometric shapes to give structure and add to the image.

True
ease in
writing comes
from art, not chance,
As those move easiest
who have learn'd
to dance

Alexander Pope

ALTERNATIVE LAYOUTS

If you have just one large word, name or sentence to letter on a page, this could be your chance to do some really dramatic calligraphy.

PASTING UP

As its name implies, a paste-up is a design rough, in which the different elements of the design are stuck down in their correct positions on one background sheet. It may be black and white or coloured and should include everything you want to appear on the final version, including text and illustrations, if there are any.

There are three basic reasons for doing a paste-up. First, as a reference for yourself during the production of a piece of work. Second, you might use one as a visual – that is, as a way of showing how the final piece of work will look to yourself or another person. Finally, a paste-up is the last stage of a piece of work before going to press, if printed.

PASTE-UPS FOR REFERENCE

Producing a paste-up is a way of seeing whether your design will work before you actually settle down to do your best copy. By writing out all the text at the intended size and with the intended nib, and producing illustrations if necessary, you can judge whether you need to make any adjustments.

Duplicating work

Pricking through (1) involves laying the paste-up over a piece of paper and pricking the paper with a pin or other sharp point to mark where each line appears. By doing this you can make a number of identical copies. Careful examination of old manuscripts will reveal that this method has been in use for centuries! It saved the scribes time and ensured that all the pages of a book

matched. The tiny holes can be hidden afterwards
by rubbing gently on the back of the paper with a
fingernail.

An alternative method is to use dividers (**2**) to transfer
measurements from the paste-up to the 'good' copy.

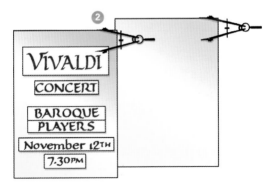

You can also make a measuring ruler (**3**) to transfer the
measurements. This consists of a piece of card which is
held against the paste-up and on which the positions of
the lines are ticked off. The 'rule' is then held against the
new copy and these positions are transferred.
Remember to keep a record of the nib sizes and colours
used.

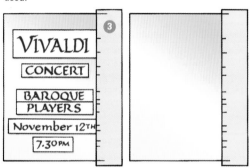

PASTE-UPS FOR CONSIDERATION
A paste-up can be used as a 'visual' – that is, a
representation of the way the finished piece of work will
appear. If you have several possible designs and cannot
decide which to use, or if you want to try the same design
with a varity of colour combinations, then make a paste-up
of each. Put them all side by side and seek a friend's
advice (or a client's opinion, if you have been asked to do
the work for someone else) so that the designs which do
not work are eliminated at this stage.

PASTE-UPS FOR PRINTING

If you have a large print run, you may decide to use the services of a professional printer; if your print run is small, however, you may find that a photocopying shop can work out cheaper. Either way you will need to produce a neat, clean, accurate paste-up. Use thick paper or board as the base for the paste-up, and protect the paste-up with a piece of tracing paper fixed over the top with tape down one side (an overlay). Use typewriter correction fluid around the edges of your pasted-down paper to avoid shadows. Test this by photocopying the paste-up.

PRINTING IN MORE THAN ONE COLOUR

Preparing work for printing in more than one colour is a slightly more complex procedure. The most common way of doing this is by separating the paste-up onto overlays, each overlay printing a different colour. A baseboard is used – usually thick card or board for the 'majority' colour (usually black); the additional pieces to be printed in colour are pasted onto transparent plastic film, hinged to one side with tape, and in register with each other.

Register marks show the exact position of the overlays relative to the baseboard. They make sure that the words and lines in each colour are printed in exactly the right place.

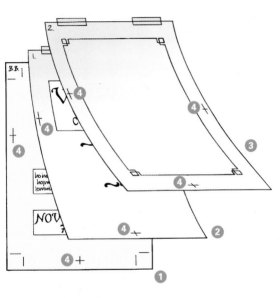

1 Baseboard: 1st colour
2 Overlay 1: 2nd colour
3 Overlay 2: 3rd colour
4 Register marks

USING COLOUR

There is one simple rule which must always be followed
when mixing paint – add the water to the paint, not vice
versa. This rule applies regardless of whether you use
tubes, jars or cakes of paint.

TRADITIONAL USE OF COLOUR

Headings and the initial letters of a stanza or verse are
often red. Vermilion and spectrum red are strong colours
which contrast dramatically when used along with
traditional black ink. Red gives warmth to your work and
claims attention, so use it on names, initials and anywhere
that you want emphasis.

**These initials look arresting
in red with black text.**

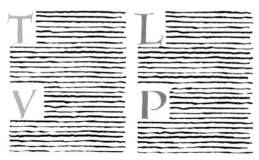

Tips and hints

- You might find it useful to keep colours such as vermilion and white in screw-top jars, just as ink is. This might encourage you to use them more.

- If you dilute some black fountain pen inks in the proportion of one part ink to three parts water you will get a gentle grey-blue tint which is very subtle and effective.

- Use the brush to measure the amount of paint you need and dilute the paint with drops of distilled water from a dropper bottle.

- A couple of smears of egg yolk in vermilion will make the colour more vibrant and add permanency.

- When working on a long piece of work, remember to add water to the paint, otherwise it will evaporate and not flow smoothly through the nib.

- Aim for a milky consistency when mixing paint, whether you're writing with a pen or simply flooding in an area with a fine sable brush.

- Reducing the length of the handle on your brushes can prevent accidents with paint, and securing palettes and ink pots with Blu Tak also helps.

The warmth of red contrasts well with the cool effect of blue and green. Alternating these three colours down a page in the traditional manner produces a balanced effect.

SOME NEWER WAYS OF USING COLOUR

In addition to using colour for initial letters, here are two more suggestions for using colour in an attractive, contemporary way.

Splattering

This can be a very effective way of decorating a humorous quotation. Use a diffuser containing waterproof ink or a watery mixture of paint (**1**). Fix the paper in a vertical position while you are working on it (**2**), but lay it flat to dry. Keep the angle of the diffuser at 90°. Don't overspray or the ink will run. Purse your lips tightly and blow long and hard (**3**). This technique can also be used to apply art fixative if you dislike using aerosols. Diffusers are readily available from art shops.

Overlapping colour

1 Choose a large nib and rule up a line template with gaps alternating from ²/₅ in (10 mm) to ¹/₁₀ in.

2 Put the template under a sheet of layout paper or other lightweight paper.

3 Using either green or blue ink, mix three bowls of tint: one watery (bowl **1**), one stronger than this but still diluted (bowl **2**), and one undiluted (bowl **3**).

4 Choose a single word which has both an ascender and a descender and write it repeatedly in the ²/₅ in (10 mm) space (this distance being the full x-height of the letters). Load your pen from the bowls in sequence

1,2,1,3,1,2,1,3,1 and so on to achieve a subtle effect.

5 Stagger the starting points of the lines and do not give the ascender its serif or the descender its final stroke.

6 Do not worry about the
overlapping of letters:
this is part of the effect of
using watery tints.

PROBLEMS IN TECHNIQUE

There are numerous problems that can arise when learning
calligraphy. The next four pages show the possible
solutions to the most likely ones.

**The stroke not sharp on
the paper**
Your forefinger or thumb
is pressing too hard and
you're not placing the nib
squarely to the paper. The
nib may need attention.
Try a few pulling strokes
on very fine sandpaper.
Finish off with a sideways
stroke once each way.
1 Too much thumb
pressure
2 Too much finger
pressure

Trouble with ink blobbing
Did you degrease the nib and the reservoir before
writing? Either lick them or pass them through a flame
to degrease. Your pen angle or the angle of the
drawing board might need adjusting. Remember that
the angle of the pen to the paper should be 90°.

The ink won't flow
This could be due to a number of causes: rusty nib
and reservoir, dirty and blocked-up nib, stale ink that

needs a few drops of distilled water, paint too thick, reservoir too tight and distorting nib, angle of pen to paper too low.

The ink 'bleeds' on the paper
Change ink or paper. Try protecting the surface with a brand solution bought from an art stockist.

The writing hand aches
You're trying too hard. RELAX. Take some refreshment, put on some soothing music, and try some pen play.

The colour smudges
Spray finished work with fixative (or even hairspray). Add a couple of drops of pure egg yolk (no white!) to the colour – too much leads to cracking later.

Back, shoulders, and knees ache
Too tense – your writing will show this tension. Check height of table, chair and writing area.

The new nib scratches
A few pulling strokes on very fine sandpaper should help. Don't be tempted to press harder. After half an hour it should be eased for you.

The letters look careless
You are using the pen like a paintbrush! Instead, use it precisely, as you would a screwdriver or a chisel and try to be more precise about starting and finishing strokes.

The letters look childlike and stiff

You're trying too hard! Check your knowledge of stroke order before you start a letter. Don't read from the book stroke by stroke.

Double letters look clumsy

Remember to create them as a pair, although this doesn't necessarily mean making them both identical. You could add a swash or flourish to one of the pair (*right*).

Certain letters always look wrong

Trace from the book the correct shape and try to *feel* what it is like to make that shape, then try again. Practise words with problem letters with a dry pen, don't avoid them. Never do a long row of them – construct words instead, and check the stroke order with the book. Also, check your writing angle.

The letters look odd
Check with the Skeleton alphabet. Are the proportions of your letters correct? Is your pen at the wrong angle? Thick and thin strokes show up this fault very clearly. Are you changing the angle?

| Too steep | Too flat | Angle changes |

The letters change size
Rule a top line for a while, either an x-height or capital height, so that you get used to the size. Practise capital letters in a short quotation.

The letters lean backward
Check your sitting position. Are your legs crossed? Is the paper in front of you, or a little to one side? This is a common occurrence with left-hand writing.

The descender of line A hits the ascender of line B
Reduce your descenders by a fraction, or leave off the last stroke, and only add it when the next line is written and space for it is there. Alternatively, leave a fraction more space between lines.

Double ascenders and descenders look odd
Play with the word and find an acceptable pattern and shape for the word. If in any doubt, keep it simple.

5. Projects

This section of the book gives several projects, all of which can be successfully completed by beginners. Finishing a piece is part of the creative process, and until something is in the post, hanging on a wall or has been given away, it has not been completely finished. Calligraphy is to be read by others and that often only happens when the piece is completely finished.

Letters, these seemingly commonplace little signs, taken for granted

More powerful than all poetry,

A B C

all science, in

I J K

are the letters of the alph

S T U V W X Y

twenty-six pillars of strength up

of creative power. They are the abstract refinements of the crea

FRAMING YOUR WORK

An experienced frame-maker will discuss suitable types of frame with you. You can also choose what mount to use from a selection of card. It's quite usual for the mount to echo one of the colours in the artwork. Delicate calligraphy does not need an elaborate frame.

This lively version of the Italic hand by Peter Thornton celebrates the joy of lettering.

LABELLING

This will give you many opportunities to use your calligraphy. Sometimes people will want your calligraphy in place of their own writing. At other times it is more appropriate to have a calligrapher than a printer.

Key points to consider when labelling

How is the label to be attached?
Is it to be written on sticky paper covered in transparent film, tied on with ribbon, stand by itself, hung up?

Clarity of message
Would colour be appropriate? Have you remembered to use different sizes of lettering, large for attention, small for detail? Have you left enough space around the message? Is the lettering in the appropriate style? Does the surface need to be protected with fixative, sealant or a cover? Is it to be framed or mounted? Have you used the correct weight of paper or card?

Size
Always work out the size your labels need to be first. Write out the words (to less than your maximum label size) in the middle of a sheet of paper and trim afterwards, centring them or positioning them as necessary.

Labelling can be used for public notices, ex libris tickets, bookmarks, room name-plates, conference plans, table place-names, filing systems, storage in the kitchen, classroom or workplace, gift tags, drink labels, simple instructions, displays of goods and many other things. Take every opportunity that presents itself, and enjoy it!

Producing labels

There are different methods for pasting-up labels, depending on whether you require one label of each type or more.

Multiple copies

These can be made by pasting up four, six or eight labels onto one sheet. Write out one neat version (**1**) and photocopy it several times, or write it out several times. Paste it up as shown (**2**). Add tiny black dots to mark the cutting lines (trim marks) before photocopying (**3**).

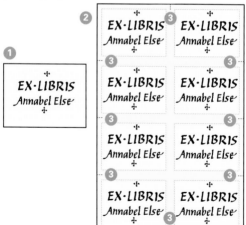

Individual copies

Draw guidelines in pencil on a large sheet of paper.
Write each label neatly, leaving plenty of space
around each one. Draw the trim marks after writing,
so that each one looks centred. Leave a double space
if making a stand-up card.

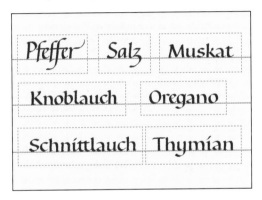

GIFTWRAP

This simple project combines two important aspects of calligraphy. First, the need to practise and get rhythm into your writing, and second, to progress to the stage where you can give your calligraphy away.

You need a 420 x 594 mm (A2) layout pad, as smaller paper isn't big enough for wrapping most presents. Don't worry about buying such a large pad, because you can always cut it down if you want to work at a smaller size. Practise with the larger nibs in your collection, and with the decorative ones. A2 paper is also a good size for working out poster designs, and for gaining confidence in using larger letters. If you do make a mistake, ignore it and continue writing, don't try to scratch it out.

Build up supplies of wrapping paper by practising Italic with a range of nibs and pens. Reduce a large design down to a small size for smaller gifts. Don't enlarge small writing as it will expose faults, whereas reduction hides them!

Instead of letters, make borders based on letters. Feel free to turn the page round as you work. Fill the whole sheet with ideas. Photocopy the best ones for future reference.

ADDING COLOUR

To filled sheets of rhythmic writing you only need to add a
dash of colour and matching ribbon to get a very
sophisticated effect.

- Colour in the counters (the inside shape of the letter)
  with felt-tip pens.
- Add lines of colour between the writing lines.
- Add gold, silver, or multicoloured stars and dots using
  stationery stickers.
- Add gold or silver with instant pens.

GIFT TAGS

Design each gift tag to match particular sheets of paper. The design does not have to replicate the wrapping paper but it should fit in with it. Use a hole puncher to make holes and silver or gold twine.

GREETINGS CARDS: HANDMADE

The one thing that a calligrapher can do with a greetings card that a printer cannot do is put the recipient's name on it. The card can be personalised by using a familiar quotation, a nickname or sharing a private joke.

Calligraphy has a lot to offer here. Use the opportunity to say something personal with a handmade card and envelope. You may find that friends ask you to make cards for occasions such as 18th and 21st birthday celebrations, retirements and other occasions when congratulations are in order. These personal communications can be very enjoyable to make (*see overleaf*).

A large version is ideal for a card which is going to be signed by many people. Indicate to them where they should write or the signatures will wander everywhere!

Suggested procedure

1 Use stiff thick paper or Fabriano HP paper (this is made with 50 per cent cotton and is quite heavy). Cut the sheet into strips, each 100 mm (4 in) deep. Draw writing lines along the length of each strip.

2 Make a pencil sketch of your idea on a strip of layout paper.

3 Fold the rough version of the design as in the diagram.

4 Write out your message on the card, leaving 30 mm (1¼ in) clear space before you begin the first letter. When you have finished, trim off all but 30 mm (1¼ in) at the other end.

5 Measure the length of the card. Divide it into folded sections. It can be in four, six or even eight sections. Make sure that the beginning of the message is on the outside.

6 Write an envelope to match the colour scheme. Use art fixative to protect the letters.

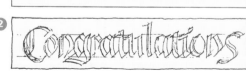

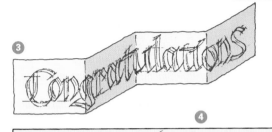

③ Congratulations

④ Congratulations

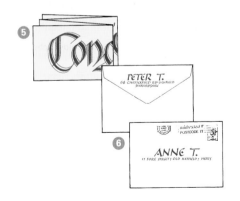

⑤ Cong

PETER T.
68 CHESTERFIELD RD·LICHFIELD
STAFFORDSHIRE

ANNE T.
17 FORE STREET · OLD HATFIELD · HERTS

GREETINGS CARDS: PRINTED

If you have any of your calligraphy reproduced, make sure you do it well, as multiple copies of a badly formed design or clumsy letters are hard to live with. Spend as much time as possible getting the details right, before going to the printer. On the other hand, do not be discouraged from trying a small print run – it's good fun, and you can learn a great deal from it.

Design tips

There are a few points you should bear in mind as you design:

- As your design will end up being pasted together, you can break it down into its elements at the beginning. This way you can concentrate on each one individually, then match them together later.

- Do a couple of photocopies of your final design before printing. This will show up any faults in positioning.

- Plan the colours at the design stage, not as an afterthought. Colours are more significant than merely brightness or contrast. Use the colour sensitively.

- Consider if you want to use paper or card to print on. This may affect the way you do the paste-up as paper needs to be folded more than card to give it stiffness.

- Use decorative pens and interesting letterforms.

- Use colour sparingly.

Add colour after printing

Work out a card design and print it in black. After
folding, add colour by hand. Keep changing the colour
so that each card is an original!

Printing on coloured paper

Print a set of cards using coloured paper or card and
then add other colours. This gives the effect of a
multicoloured print run.

Finishing touches

Cards can be printed in black and have finishing
touches made by hand afterwards. This gives the effect
of being a handmade card. Use gold and silver pens,
and paint.

Copyright

You should not write out a modern poem or quotation
and sell your design without checking the copyright.
You may have to pay a fee to the copyright holder.

Paper or card?

If your design is being printed onto paper, then use it
folded twice (**a**). If on card then fold once only (**b**). This
way you will get one paper card per sheet with the
message printed inside, or two card greetings cards per
sheet (the inside will be blank). Check the final size with
your envelope size.

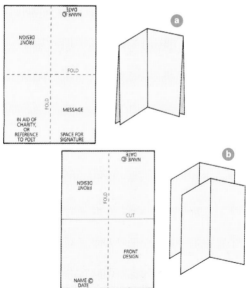

SPECIAL OCCASIONS

This project is as much about organisation as it is about calligraphy. A wedding or similar occasion is an ideal opportunity for you to use your calligraphy. Printing and handwriting names combine to make this a big project, but you don't have to do it all at once. If you feel daunted by the idea of doing invitations, menus, placecards and seating plans, just think of them as centred lists or labels.

The flexibility of Italic makes it ideal for this project, and you can play with a few flourishes if you like. People are often delighted when they see their names beautifully written, and it may be the first time they've seen what design lies within it. One or two ideas are given here, but only use them as starting points. You'll find that new ideas come to you as you go along.

INVITATIONS

These are traditionally centred (*see pages 76–79*). Use a larger nib for the name of the celebrating person or couple and leave extra space around it to help people focus on it. You might add a design or use a colour appropriate to the occasion itself.

Your printer will be able to advise you on weight of card and colour effects. When you have completed your design, mount it on card to protect it.

If you work to a size larger than the final printed size, then bear in mind what effect the reduction process during printing will have. Generally speaking, it's a good idea to work slightly larger, but check with the printer.

Hints and tips

- Always check the details with the hosts before going to press.
- Ask the printer for a sample of the card so that you can try writing on it.
- Make sure that the pen does not snag and that the ink does not 'bleed' into the card too much.
- Try to obtain a typed guest list to work from, to avoid mistakes.
- If you use paint, remember to protect the words with fixative after writing.

MENUS

Menus are usually done some time after the invitations, and you may like to do them in the same style to give an impression of unity. Make sure you check the spelling with the manager of the venue. A pleasing effect can be obtained by matching the colour schemes, lettering or design of the invitations, or by adding the same motif throughout.

PLACECARDS

The name of each guest can be written on a small stand-up card. You may like to add a motif or illustration, or match the colour of the ink with the table decorations, flowers or linen.

M·E·N·U

Pâtés au Gratin Portugaise

Carré d'Agneau Rôti au Romarin
Pommes Parisienne
Panaché de Legumes

Bombe Glacé Orange Nassau

Etienne

SEATING PLAN

This is done as a list, one for each letter of the alphabet. They are written out on separate sheets of card and then mounted on large sheets of background card. The reason for breaking it up in this way is that if you do go wrong, it only affects a very small part of the overall plan and can easily be redone.

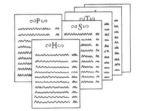

When all the lists are done, lay them on the floor on top of the background card and play with the arrangement until you find one you like. Use a set square or a T-square to keep them straight. When you have decided on the final layout, mark the corners of each list with a pin prick and then stick them down one by one.

DESIGNING POSTERS

Posters are fun to do, but never underestimate how long it takes to make a successful design: you will need to make several changes before you achieve a good result. If some handmade posters are required, a few shortcuts are worth knowing. If your design is for print you can cut and paste to get it just right. Either way you will want to display good letterforms and use space and colour to arrest people's attention. Write out the various pieces of information and play around with them until the positions look right; tape in position and ask others for their comments. Make final adjustments and write out one for final approval; then mass-produce them.

Points to consider

- Use a grid to help you align information vertically as well as horizontally. This can either be a pattern you have drawn yourself or you can just put a piece of squared or graph paper under your sheet of layout paper so that the lines show through and act as a guide.

- Make plenty of rough thumbnail sketches of various ideas before you start to write out the calligraphy.

- Don't be afraid to edit the information and check the spellings.

- Check that the text gives all the necessary information. What? Where? When? Why? How much? Who? Try showing a rough sketch to a friend – they will have a more objective view than you, and may be able to spot errors and omissions.

- Have more paper available than you need, and be prepared to waste some experimenting with colour and pen size. If you can't decide which of your sketches has the most potential, look at them in a mirror. This enables you to judge which one arrests your attention when you are not distracted by reading.

- Work as large as possible. You can photocopy the design, reducing it for use as handbills. If you need handbills but find that your poster loses too much in the reduction process, then do a simple design at the smaller size.

- Use colours appropriately. Don't ignore the potential of black and white which can be very arresting in a busy environment.

- If you feel the poster needs some illustration, add logos, motifs and drawings. If you don't draw, trace a picture or use a silhouette. Alternatively, ask an artist to help you. Children's art can work very well too.

- Sometimes people will not display a large poster as they look intrusive, so several smaller ones may work better. They can be used singly or in multiples.

- Posters generally need to be protected from the weather if used outdoor in public places. This can be done by spraying, covering with transparent film, or by putting them into a frame.

PRODUCING POSTERS

HANDMADE

If you need only one or two posters then making them by hand is the best way. Printing is economical only when quantities are needed. The major advantage of making a number of posters by hand is that they can all be slightly different, with varying coloured elements or decoration, and yet still be the same basic design. There are lots of things to do which will add interest to your design:

Hints and tips

- Make stencils and cut out motifs or individual letters from card, paper or felt. Stick them on, creating a collage effect.

- Write out your letters in outline and flood in with colour, or pattern them.

- Spray, stipple and blot colour on your work.

- Add rubbings and other interesting textures. These ideas can complement your basic calligraphic designs and make each poster quite individual.

- When you have completed one good paste-up, lay it over several sheets of the paper you are using for your poster, and prick through the positions of the writing lines, and beginnings and endings of large letters. This saves a lot of time and avoids inaccuracies arising when you want all copies to match each other.

This theatre poster is a good example
of an effective handmade poster.

PRINTED POSTERS

Having posters printed offers options. Colour is expensive to print, but if you use coloured paper and black print, you achieve a colourful effect at minimal cost. Long print runs are cost effective and free your energies to concentrate on the design quality.

Preparing for print

- Photocopying is the cheapest method of printing for a print run of up to 500 copies. The largest size most photocopying shops have is 11 x 14 in (A3).

- You can use black and white most effectively and add colour by hand afterward. Splattering, streaking, using coloured washes and sticking on coloured paper are possible ways of doing this. A black and white poster stuck on a coloured background can be effective.

- The real bonus of a print run is that you can reduce your lettering, motifs and logos when you are pasting up.

- Good lettering on a simple design will convey information clearly. It is therefore a good idea to concentrate on the quality of the lettering rather than on over-elaborate design.

- You need not conform to the tradition of making posters portrait shape (upright).

Sizes and proportion

Work twice as large as your final design. Reducing the size minimises unevenness in your writing. Also, you can print twice or four times as many small posters for the same price as large posters. Bear in mind that many people are unwilling to display large posters, so have plenty of smaller versions to hand.

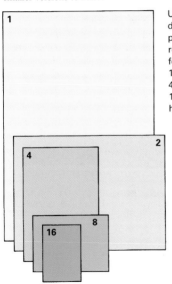

Use the same design as the posters but reduce the size for handbills – 1 large poster = 4 small posters = 16 leaflets or handbills.

EXHIBITION POSTERS

These two posters solve the problem of presenting the reader with a list. In each case the answer was to use capitals closely stacked and plenty of space.

A list which has a straight left-hand margin (left justified) is easier to construct than one which is right justified.

Centring and right justifying both need to be pasted up, whereas left justifying only needs the length of the longest line to be found. That distance is then measured in from the right-hand side, and the resulting point is where the lettering can start from.

POETRY AND PROSE

Writing out any text requires a certain amount of planning – a fact which may not be obvious when looking at the finished piece! Good writing needs rhythm, sharpness and a sense of freedom. You can achieve this if you plan everything before you begin your final version. The next six pages show how to plan and use thumbnail sketches to choose the best layout.

A simple shape that connects with the meaning of the text can have a striking effect, as shown in this example by Ieuan Rees.

Planning a layout

- First, consider the meaning of the poem, quotation or piece of prose. Check spelling, author and punctuation. Then decide which letterform most suits the text.

- Make some thumbnail sketches using handwriting (*see pages 146–147*). Always draw a shape around your ideas.

- Write out your text using different-sized nibs and capitals for some sections. Use a larger nib but same-size letters for pieces you want to emphasise; this is an alternative to using capitals. Photocopy your layout at this stage if you can.

- Do a paste-up. Adjust anything which needs to be changed and consider weight and balance carefully. Is there harmony in your colour scheme? Does it all hang together well? Above all, can it be easily read?

- When you're satisfied with your paste-up, use a pin to prick through where lines are to be drawn. Rule up on best paper and write it out. Refer to your final paste-up whenever you wish. When your work is dry, begin finding the edges of your piece by moving four long strips of card around the sides. Leave as much space as you can around the piece, in order to set off the words.

ASSESSING THUMBNAIL SKETCHES

A thumbnail sketch is a rough, usually smaller, version of what the finished piece will look like. Making several thumbnails allows you to compare one with another, notice possible improvements, and choose the best version or combination of versions.

1 Written this way round it becomes too staccato. It's a good idea, but does not work for this particular quotation.
2 A large initial overpowers the three lines.
3 Has possibilities.

4 Simple – but the shape is very long. And also the author's name has been missed out.

5 The capitals certainly draw the reader's attention. Worth writing out a second time; balance the weight of lines 1 and 4 with lines 2 and 3.

6 Similar to **3**; must watch how lines sit under one another.

④

most people would succeed in small things,
if they were not troubled by great ambitions.

⑤

MOST PEOPLE
would succeed in small things
if they were not troubled by
GREAT AMBITIONS

LONGFELLOW

⑥

most people
    would succeed in small things
if they were not troubled by
        great ambitions. LONGFELLOW

TOWARDS THE FINAL VERSION

From the various thumbnail sketches, two ideas have been developed further. In the first version (**a**, *opposite*) the capitals do not relate to the rest of the text. It is as if they are shouting at the reader.

In the second version (**b**, *below*) the lines need to be rearranged to form a harmonious shape. Nevertheless this one would seem to be the most effective. Often, simple ideas are best.

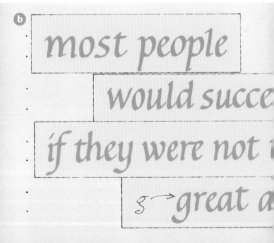

a

MOST PEOPLE *no 3 WM. Pen.*

would succeed in small things

if they were not troubled by

GREAT AMBITIONS

LONGFELLOW

no 3½ W.M. Pen

d in small things $

oubled by

bitions LONGFELLOW

6. More Difficult Letterforms

Once you have mastered the three basic letterforms, you may like to try one or more of the more difficult letterforms shown here – Copperplate, Uncial and Gothic.

COPPERPLATE

Copperplate is a general term for a family of Roundhand writing styles introduced by Gianfrancesco Cresci of Milan in 1560. This new style was flowing and looped and the pen was not lifted from the paper. It suited the new printing method of engraving onto a copperplate, from which it took its name. It is used when a formal look is needed.

For Copperplate writing you need a flexible pointed nib and the technique is to apply controlled pressure on the *downward* strokes. Much practice is needed, not only to acquaint yourself with the ornate letterforms, but also to gain experience of the pressure technique with the nib.

Ladder and pen angle
The hand has an x-height about 7 thick strokes of the nib. Ascenders and descenders are 3 x-heights when looped, less when straight. Capitals are at least

3 x-heights. Numerals are 10–11 nib widths. The pen is held at 55° to the horizontal. These dimensions are only a guide but in all cases the steep pen angle of 55° is constant. Apply pressure to open the nib when measuring the x-height. Ink reservoirs are inappropriate as they restrict flexibility.

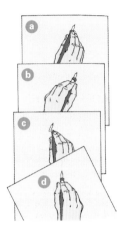

Hand, pen and paper positions
a Right handed 55° angle.
b Left handed 55° angle.
c Elbow joint pen designed to help right handers.
d Adjusting the paper position also helps you write at 55° to the writing line.

Strokes
There are four strokes for Copperplate:
1 Part of the letter is formed with hairlines as the nib travels across the paper.
2 When pressure is applied the nib widens and forms swells that begin and end in hairlines.
3 Some strokes have square ends.
4 Hairlines joining letters are known as ligatures.

Round

COPPERPLATE MAJUSCULES

COPPERPLATE MAJUSCULES

COPPERPLATE MINUSCULES

nopqrstuvwx

nopqrstuvwx

567890.

567890

UNCIAL LETTERFORM

The Uncial letterform is extremely ancient; similar letterforms existed in Greece several centuries BC. In the 4th century AD its influence increased in the Roman Empire because it was used for many Christian writings and manuscripts and it became the main book hand. The name Uncial derives from *uncia*, meaning an inch, the height of the earliest examples.

Uncials are formed with full, round counters (spaces) within the letters. They were derived from the square Roman capitals, but were far more suited to rapid writing.

Examples of Uncial forms

1 The first Uncial alphabets emerged as an alternative to the Rustica (informal) capitals (*see page 176*); 4th-century capitals were of an even height, usually an inch.

2 Half-Uncials show the beginning of our lower-case forms in their ascenders and descenders.

3 *The Book of Kells* shows the Insular Uncial script, an Irish interpretation of Uncial and Half-Uncial.

True Uncial is a capital form contained within two
guidelines only, with minimal ascenders and descenders,
but this was followed by Half-Uncial, the precursor of
most minuscule forms. In Half-Uncial certain letters break
the top and bottom lines, beginning to form ascenders and
descenders as we know them in lower-case letters. Uncials
and Half-Uncials remained popular until the end of the
8th century, when the Carolingian form swept Europe (*see
page 177*).

MODERN UNCIAL

Derived from the traditional Uncials, the modern form keeps the spirit of the letter with its chunky serifs and flattened round counters. All antiquated letterforms such as A F G H M are abandoned and the modern versions are used. Vertical strokes are a little lighter and serifs have a diagonal rather than horizontal top line. Finishing strokes taper away to the left. Many advertisers and graphic designers use Modern Uncial freely in their work.

Tools

Most wide-nibbed pens and chisel-ended brushes can be used for forming Uncial letterforms. Pens will give the clearest outline, but brushes can produce a rather attractive softer feel. Chisel-tipped felt pens will also produce a good Uncial form, although they need to be as wide as possible.

This example shows how Modern Uncials give a piece of writing a Celtic image.

Ladder and pen angle
The hand has an x-height of 3½–4 nib widths.
Ascenders and descenders are 5–6 nib widths. The
hand is written with the pen at 15° to the horizontal.

MODERN UNCIAL alphabet

F c h i j k L

F c h i j k L

N O P Q R

N O P Q R

x y z

x y z

BASIC GOTHIC

There was a powerful economic reason for the
introduction of Gothic letters. Increased production of
books had led to a shortage of vellum and parchment and
therefore an increase in cost. Calligraphers had to get
more writing on each page! For this reason Gothic has
little space between lines, the letters are tightly packed and
the penforms are angular – even the o has corners. For
further compactness, ascenders and descenders are short
and letters are compressed, sometimes to the point of
sharing a common stem. Abbreviations are widely used.

Ladder and pen angle
The hand has an x-height of 5 nib widths. Capitals
are 6 nib widths. Ascenders and descenders are 7
nib widths. The hand is written with the pen at 45°
to the horizontal (90° for hairlines).

It is the compactness on the page which gives Gothic writing its nickname 'Black Letter'. The density of a page of Gothic is enlivened by the use of vermilion majuscules, whose roundness contrasts with the angularity of the minuscules. However, both majuscules and minuscules are difficult to read unless they are carefully spaced.

Spacing minuscules
The basic stroke is the letter i. Aim to balance white space with black mark. Check your work by turning it upside down. Words should resemble a set of railings.

Gothic serifs and majuscules
Turn your wide pen 90° to the writing to make Gothic serifs and majuscules. Use a double stroke automatic pen or another large nib to build up the majuscules.

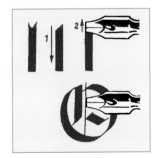

BASIC GOTHIC MAJUSCULES

BASIC GOTHIC MINUSCULES

g h i j k l m

g h i j k l m

s t u v w w

s t u v w w

VARIATIONS OF GOTHIC

There are many Gothic variations. You need one that was originally a penform, not a typeface, to study and copy. Legibility is most important, so avoid ornate versions such as the Textura shown overleaf when writing a long text.

There are only a few opportunities to use Gothic calligraphy. When they occur give yourself some time to revise your knowledge of the letterforms. Only time will

build up the confidence that will give you the regular rhythm that Gothic requires.

Dürer's Gothic

Gothic capitals designed by Albrecht Dürer in the early 16th century are not easy to learn, but are very lively. They contrast with his traditional Textura Gothic minuscules which tend to be very formal and regular.

Textura Gothic

With Textura the 'basic' stroke is, in fact, three individual strokes which means you write slowly and lift the pen more often than with other Gothic hands. This Textura Quadrata script was written in France in the early 14th century. The letters have a rhythm which prevents the page looking heavy and dull. The fine hairlines are achieved by turning the nib onto a corner and using little or no pressure on the pen.

A B C

K L M

T U V

a b c d e

p q r s t

1 2 3 4 5

DEFGHIJ

NOPQRS

WXYZ

fghijklmno

uvwxyz

67890

A BRIEF HISTORY OF WRITING

In a book like this it is not possible to present a detailed history of writing; we can only briefly introduce a fascinating subject.

While people have used marks and signs for tens of thousands of years, we can only trace our historical scripts back for about 3000 years to the Phoenicians, who used a script based on 22 letters, some of which we would recognise today. Their alphabet was taken up by the Greeks and then by the Romans who adopted it and spread it across the Western world. Any European-

Earliest alphabet
Phoenician letters from the Moabite or Mesha Stone, dated to 842 BC. The writing ran from right to left.

language speaker looking at a Roman inscription will recognise the symbols, even though he may not understand the words. There was nothing inevitable about this; the symbols have survived because they are convenient to use.

EARLY ROMAN LETTERS

Examine a Roman inscription carved out of stone and you will see capital letters only. Big, graceful and square, they were well suited for use on inscriptions. However, they would not have been an ideal written hand because they were slow and exacting.

Roman monumental
Roman capitals on the tombstone of Gaius Valerius Victor (*below*), standard bearer of Legion II Augusta at Isca (Caerleon), South Wales, after AD 74.

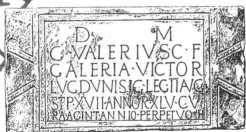

RUSTICA

The Romans needed an everyday writing style for letters written on papyrus using a square-ended reed pen. It was a compressed style because writing materials were expensive, but it was a flowing style because it needed to be written quickly.

UNCIALS

Improvements in writing implements led to the adoption of Uncial as the favoured script of Western Europe. Its rounded letters were quicker to write than Rustica, a factor of increasing significance as the spread of Christianity led to an ever-growing demand for Bibles and religious texts which were copied by monastic scribes.

Half-Uncials were a further development. Within this hand there began to emerge the ascenders and descenders that we now associate with lower-case letters. It was the forerunner of all of today's minuscule letters.

Church writing

Uncial script from ecclesiastical regulations in Latin, 6th or 7th century.

CAROLINGIAN

As Western Europe broke up, consistency in scripts across Europe was lost. Local regions developed their own hands and, although many were clearly derived from Uncials and Half-Uncials, there were considerable variations. Shortly before AD 800 there arose a new European leader in Charlemagne who, although he could not read, was shrewd enough to recognise the power of the written word. He decided to re-establish standard letterforms.

Named after him, the Carolingian form was the first true minuscule hand. It established itself as the formal bookhand in Europe and survived in that role for nearly 300 years. It was one of the most significant developments in the history of writing and its influence on today's printed material is still apparent.

Carolingian Renaissance

Very early Carolingian form from a Salzburg manuscript of Alcuin's letters, written 798–99. Alcuin of York was the powerhouse of the Carolingian Renaissance.

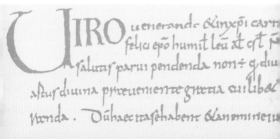

GOTHIC

The Middle Ages brought increased demands for
documents with secular purposes. They led to a severe
shortage of vellum and to a consequent sharp increase in
its price. There emerged the need for a hand which was as
quick to write as the Carolingian, but which was
sufficiently dense to make economical use of the available
vellum. The answer to the problem was Gothic, a neat
compressed style which sacrificed roundness and cut short
ascenders and descenders in order to get as much text as
possible onto a page. The hand was used across Northern
Europe with many regional variations.

Northern Gothic

Gothic Textura from the Kinloss or Boswell Psalter,
Cistercian Abbey of Kinloss, Scotland c.1500.

ROTUNDA

Though most of Europe adopted a standard Gothic form,
Italy showed a marked resistance. There, a compromise
style was adopted between Gothic and other earlier forms.
It is known as Rotunda.

Rotunda
From a Florentine liturgical text, c.1500.

ITALIC

The Renaissance began in Italy and had a profound effect upon calligraphy. Gothic was swept away and back came the stylish influences of Carolingian. The script bloomed into Italic, a family of hands that re-established elegance. The style emerged in the 15th century just as the first printing presses were appearing and was promptly adopted for use in typography. It has remained for over 500 years as part of a popular repertoire of type.

Venetian Italic
Italic from the regulations to be kept by the Procurators of the Basilica of St Mark, Venice, written by the priest John, 1558.

COPPERPLATE

While Italic remained part of the
typographer's stock in trade, hand
scripts moved on. The arrival of
the quilled pen allowed scribes to
mimic what had once been a style
of copper engravers. While similar
to Italic in its elegance, Copperplate
has a fine gradation in line
thickness which encourages style
and ornamentation. Copperplate
or Roundhand soon became the
accepted hand and lasted into
the 20th century. However, before that, the
quill had long been replaced by the metal pens used
by many of our parents and grandparents.

FOUNDATIONAL HAND

Towards the end of the 19th century William Morris
(1834–1896), whose interest lay in medieval designs,
created the Arts and Crafts Movement in England as a
reaction to mass-produced products. Morris had a direct
influence upon Edward Johnston (1872–1944) who,
having studied old manuscripts at the British Museum,
became fascinated by the tools and techniques used to
provide them. He rediscovered the old skills used in
creating various letterforms and went on to teach them
to a new generation of calligraphers. To facilitate his
teaching, Johnston developed his own calligraphic hand.
This he called the Foundational hand. He based it on the
Carolingian letterforms in the 10th-century Anglo-Saxon
Ramsay Psalter.

Eighteenth-century Copperplate
Copperplate by Joseph Champion from George
Bickham's *The Universal Penman*, 1743.

the Honble the Sub

Governor, and D

abcdefgh

Foundational hand
A basic teaching hand and the
ideal alphabet to start calligraphy.

MODERN DEVELOPMENTS

In 1906 Edward Johnston published what has become the
basic reference manual for calligraphers – *Writing,
Illuminating and Lettering*. It is full of practical advice on
how to make letterforms and how to design books and
manuscripts. Today, printing has been revolutionised by
the use of computers, and once again many people have
reacted by taking up a broad-edged pen to learn the art of
traditional penmanship.

GUIDELINES

These guidelines can be simply traced off, or photocopied, and extended. If you enlarge or reduce them, you get a set of lines to work with nibs of various sizes.

Guidelines for Foundational
Using Osmiroid B4 fountain pen.

Guidelines for Foundational
Using Osmiroid B3 fountain pen.

Basic Italic
Using Osmiroid B4 fountain pen.

Italic
5° slant

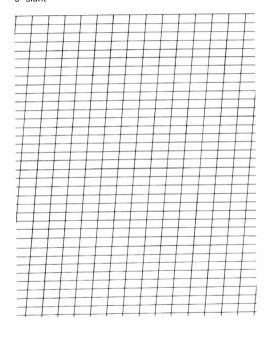

Copperplate

Basic Gothic
Using Osmiroid B4 fountain pen.

Glossary

Alignment An arrangement of lines of lettering in relation to their margins.

Ascenders The parts of lower-case letters extending above the x-height.

Baseline The lower guideline of a letter's x-height.

Centred Lines of lettering arranged around a symmetrical axis.

Counter The space enclosed or defined by the curve or stroke of a letter.

Cursive A 'running' hand in which the letters are joined up, for example, Italic handwriting.

Descenders The parts of lower-case letters extending below the x-height.

Flourishes Ribbon-like pen strokes used with Italic lettering.

Foundational hand Edward Johnston's teaching script, developed from traditional sources.

Guidelines Faint lines drawn to help the calligrapher to do an even line of lettering.

Illumination The process of decorating manuscripts. It literally means to 'light up' a manuscript by the use of raised gold (gilding).

Indent An extra space left at the beginning of a line of lettering.

Initial The first letter of a piece of work or of a verse, often coloured and decorated or illuminated in manuscripts.

Italic A generic term meaning a writing form developed in Italy, characterised by its slant and cursiveness.

Justified Lines of lettering that have even margins at the right- and left-hand edges.

Layout The arrangement of design elements on a page or paper.

Ligature The small joining line between two letters in a word.

Lower case A small or minuscule letter.

Margins The borders of paper left around areas of lettering.

Majuscules Capital letters. *See upper case.*

Minuscules Calligraphic term for 'little' letters. *See lower case.*

Monoline Letters without thick and thin strokes. For example, Skeleton letters and any letters written with a ballpoint or 'roller ball' pen.

Parchment Inner skins of sheep or pigs, prepared for writing.

Pen angle The angle between the writing line and the thinnest stroke of a broad-edged pen. For example, Foundational hand is written with a writing angle of 30°, Italic with an angle of 45°.

Serif A small finishing stroke for letter strokes.

Stress The angle of the thickest stroke in a letterform.

Swashes Extended strokes on letters which convey elegance.

Thumbnail sketches A first draft for a text. A pencil or ballpoint pen may be used for this set of sketches to explore opportunities.

Upper case Typographic term for capital letters, also called majuscules. Upper and lower case refer to the flat trays (cases) in which printers used to store metal pieces of type.

Vellum Calf skin or goat skin prepared for writing. Expensive and very beautiful to write on.

Weight The 'heaviness' or 'boldness' of letters. Determined by the height of the letter in relation to the width of the nib used.

X-height The height of lower-case letters excluding the ascenders or descenders.

Index

COLLINS GEM
BABIES'
names
a
?
z
a mine of information

COLLINS GEM
BEER
a mine of information

COLLINS GEM
BIRDS
a mine of information

COLLINS GEM
CALORIE
Counter
a mine of information

COLLINS GEM
FACT FILE
?
a mine of information

COLLINS GEM
FENG SHUI
a mine of information

COLLINS GEM
FLAGS
a mine of information

COLLINS GEM
Healthy
EATING
a mine of information

COLLINS GEM
QUOTATIONS
"
a mine of information

COLLINS GEM
SAS
Self-Defence
a mine of information

COLLINS GEM
SAS
Survival Guide
a mine of information

COLLINS GEM
SEASHORE
a mine of information

COLLINS GEM
TREES
a mine of information

COLLINS GEM
Understanding
DREAMS
a mine of information

COLLINS GEM
WILD
flowers
a mine of information

COLLINS GEM
WINE
Dictionary
a mine of information